BIG GIANT,
LITTLE BEAR
TWO FOLKTALES FROM THE ARCTIC

Retold by Rosalind Kerven
Illustrated by Frances Castle

THE GIANT

An old tale from the Inuit people of northern Canada

Scamblesby CE Primary
School
Scamblesby
Louth
Lincs
LN11 9XG

Tel No: 01507 343629

Turn to page 21 for LITTLE BEAR

Published by Pearson Education Limited, Edinburgh Gate, Harlow, Essex, CM20 2JE.

www.pearsonschools.co.uk

Text © Rosalind Kerven 2013
Designed by Bigtop
Original illustrations © Frances Castle 2013
Illustrated by Frances Castle, Arena Illustration

The right of Rosalind Kerven to be identified as author of this work has been asserted by her in accordance with the Copyright, Designs and Patents Act 1988.

First published 2013

21

10

British Library Cataloguing in Publication Data
A catalogue record for this book is available from the British Library

ISBN 978 0435 14372 5

Copyright notice
All rights reserved. No part of this publication may be reproduced in any form or by any means (including photocopying or storing it in any medium by electronic means and whether or not transiently or incidentally to some other use of this publication) without the written permission of the copyright owner, except in accordance with the provisions of the Copyright, Designs and Patents Act 1988 or under the terms of dicence issued by the Copyright Licensing Agency, Saffron House, 6–10 Kirby Street, London EC1N 8TS (www.cla.co.uk). Applications for the copyright owner's written permission should be addressed to the publisher.

Printed in Great Britain by Ashford Colour Press Ltd

Acknowledgements
We would like to thank Bangor Central Integrated Primary School, Northern Ireland; Bishop Henderson Church of England Primary School, Somerset; Bletchingdon Parochial Church of England Primary School, Oxfordshire; Brookside Community Primary School, Somerset; Bude Park Primary School, Hull; Cheddington Combined School, Buckinghamshire; Dair House Independent School, Buckinghamshire; Deal Parochial School, Kent; Glebe Infant School, Gloucestershire; Henley Green Primary School, Coventry; Lovelace Primary School, Surrey; Our Lady of Peace Junior School, Slough; Tackley Church of England Primary School, Oxfordshire; and Twyford Church of England School, Buckinghamshire for their invaluable help in the development and trialling of the Bug Club resources.

Every effort has been made to contact copyright holders of material reproduced in this book. Any omissions will be rectified in subsequent printings if notice is given to the publishers.

CHAPTER 1

A NASTY SURPRISE!

One winter's evening, a man went out fishing in the moonlight.

He walked to the middle of the ice, made a hole in it and dropped his line down. As he waited for a fish to bite, he heard the sound of footsteps crunching over the ice.

He whirled round … and saw an evil, man-eating GIANT striding towards him!

Oh no! He's coming to kill me! the man thought. *He's so big, I'll never be able to fight him off!* Then he remembered something. *Giants are supposed to be really stupid. Maybe I can escape this one with a trick.*

He thought hard. *I know. I'll pretend I'm dead already.*

So he slumped down onto the ice.

WUMP! WUMP! WUMP!

The giant strode closer and closer. He reached the man and bent down to sniff him, licking his lips greedily.

"Yummy!" he roared. "A tasty dead man — ready for my wife's cooking pot!"

He grabbed the man and flung him over his shoulder. Then he turned and strode back the way he had come.

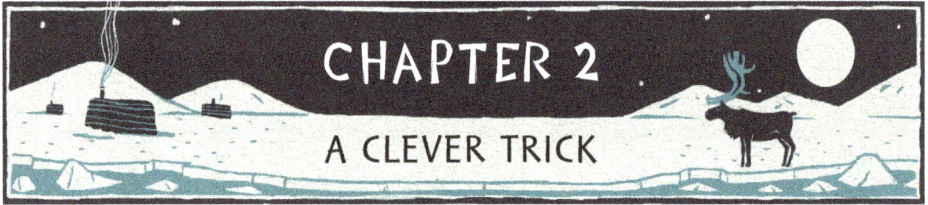

The giant hurried along over the ice. Dangling over the giant's back, the man was bumped about terribly. Nevertheless, he managed to keep utterly still. He breathed so softly that the giant couldn't hear him.

On and on they went, through the white, moonlit, frozen world. The man's heart was pounding like a stick beating a drum.

Soon they came to a clump of willow bushes, with bare twigs pushing up darkly through the deep snow. The man had a clever idea.

He reached out, grabbed one of the bushes and clung to it with all his might.

The giant tried to take another stride but he couldn't, because the man was clinging so tightly to the bush. The giant roared with frustration, pulling and struggling. He didn't realise that it was the man holding him back. He panted and cursed and tugged ...

Then suddenly the man let go.

The surprised giant staggered forward ... and tumbled over onto his nose!

"OW!" he roared. He got up and stomped on angrily.

Every time they passed some bushes the man played the same trick.

Soon, the giant was bruised all over, and exhausted from his struggles. The man couldn't stop grinning.

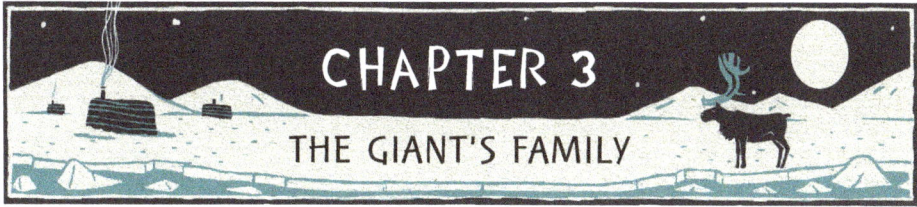

By the time they reached the giant's house, the giant was so tired he could hardly walk. His wife, a very plump giantess, waddled out to greet him.

"Look what I've brought home for our dinner," said the giant proudly. The giant showed the man to his wife. The man bravely held his breath, still acting as if he were dead.

"Mmm, he looks delicious," said the giantess, smacking her lips. "Take him inside. I'll fetch some driftwood for the fire, so I can cook him."

She shuffled away. The exhausted giant dragged the man through the entrance tunnel and put him carefully on the floor. Then he lay down on the sleeping-bench and began to snore.

Once the man was sure the giant was asleep,
he opened his eyes, ready to make his escape.
However, when he peered around, he saw ...
two giant-children staring right back at him!

"Father!" the giant-girl cried. "That man you brought back for our dinner is still alive!"

The giant turned over.

"Nonsense," he grunted. "He's as dead as driftwood."

"He's not," said the giant-boy. "We just saw him open his eyes!"

"Don't be silly," said the giant. "He dropped dead with fright as soon as he saw me." He yawned loudly and went back to sleep.

"I don't want to stay in here with that man-creature," said the giant-girl.

"Nor do I," the giant-boy agreed. "Come on, let's go outside and play."

So they crawled quickly out through the entrance tunnel.

Here's my chance! thought the man.

CHAPTER 4
MAGIC!

The man could hear the giant-children laughing outside. As their voices faded away into the distance, he sneaked through the tunnel and out of the house.

He stood up and began to run across the ice. But he had not got very far before someone behind him yelled, "STOP!"

He looked back — and groaned. The giantess was running after him!

Her legs are so long! thought the man. *She'll catch me up in no time. I'll have to play another trick. I wonder if I could work some MAGIC!*

He pulled his axe from his belt, flung it onto the frozen ground and muttered a secret word.

As the axe landed, the ice cracked open. The crack filled with water. The water gushed and bubbled. Soon it turned into a deep, rushing, foaming river.

The man was standing on one side of it —
and the giantess was stranded on the far side.

"I'm stuck!" the furious giantess yelled. "It's
too deep even for me. How can I get across?"

"Why don't you make a path through the
river by drinking the water?" the cunning man
shouted back.

The giantess knelt down on the riverbank and began to lap at the foaming water, like a dog.

"I'm doing what you said, but it's not getting any lower," she yelled.

"That's because you need to drink the whole river to make it work!" the man shouted back.

Lap-lap-lap-lap-lap went the giantess.
She drank and drank and drank ...
until she was filled with so much water
that suddenly, WHOOSH! she exploded
– and turned into a great, spreading
cloud of fog!

The fog blanked out the moonlight and drifted over the ice. The man couldn't see a thing but he waited patiently on the far side of the river.

Very soon a wind blew up. It swept away the river and the giants' house. It swept away the fog.

Now the ice was clearly lit by moonlight again. The man hurried home, chuckling as he thought about his cunning escape.

LITTLE BEAR

An old tale from the
Inuit people of Greenland

CHAPTER 1

A PRESENT FOR GRANDMOTHER

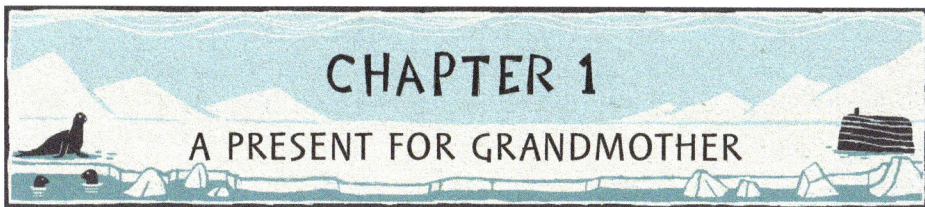

There was once an old woman who lived all by herself. The other people in the village were very kind to her and everyone called her "Grandmother".

Whenever the men went out to hunt wild animals, they always brought her some meat to cook over her fire. One day they killed a big polar bear and its cub.

"Let's give the cub to Grandmother," they said. "Its meat will be nice and tender for her to eat, and she can make herself some lovely warm clothes from its soft fur."

Grandmother was very pleased with the cub.
It was frozen stiff, so she put it by her fire to
thaw.

Her house was so cosy that it didn't take long
for the cub to warm up ... and then she got
a big surprise. The cub started to twitch! She
looked closer and saw that it was breathing.

"You're still alive!" cried Grandmother. "Oh, you poor little creature — the hunters have killed your mother!"

Then Grandmother had a wonderful idea. *I'll adopt him*, she thought. *Then I'll have a family of my own — and so will the cub.*

She took the cub in her arms and rocked him gently until he opened his eyes and gazed at her. "Hello, Little Bear," she said softly. "Are you hungry now?"

She offered him some melted seal-blubber and
he licked it greedily from her hand. Then she fed
him tiny nibbles of roast meat.

When Little Bear had eaten his fill, she let him
snuggle up next to her on the sleeping-bench.

Grandmother and Little Bear were very happy together.

Little Bear was as clever as a dog and quickly learned to understand what Grandmother said to him. In turn, she learned Little Bear's special sounds and movements. For instance, when he was hungry he would snuffle until she gave him some food.

Everyone in the village grew to love Little
Bear. Grandmother taught him to keep his claws
in so he couldn't hurt anyone. The children
thought of him as their best friend and had
great fun playing with him. The hunters decided
they would not kill any more bears.

The days went by. Little Bear grew and grew
until one day Grandmother said, "Little Bear,
you're too big to play with the children now."

Little Bear looked sad. However, he soon cheered up when Grandmother said, "The hunters need your help, Little Bear. They know how clever bears are at hunting seals. They want you to help them catch seals to feed the village children."

Little Bear was so excited that he could help the men! He danced round and round the house.

Grandmother made him a collar plaited from strips of animal skin and tied it round his neck.

"Always wear this," she said. "Then if you meet any strange people, they will realise that you are tame, so they won't hurt you. In return, always remember to treat humans gently."

Little Bear listened solemnly. Grandmother knew that he would not let her down.

Little Bear was a brilliant hunter. He went out eagerly every day, no matter how bad the weather was. He learned to stay on the right side of the wind, and to move softly. He killed his prey quickly and cleanly so that they did not feel any pain.

He brought home so much
delicious meat that the village
children grew stronger and
healthier than they had ever
been before.

Everyone was very happy,
until one day something
upsetting happened.

CHAPTER 3

LITTLE BEAR'S NEW ADVENTURE

Little Bear was out with the hunters when they met a stranger – a nasty man who lived in a distant village.

"Why does that bear wear a collar?" the stranger snarled.

"He's our Grandmother's pet," the hunters answered. "He helps us."

The stranger guffawed. He strode up to Little Bear and poked him in the belly.

Little Bear growled indignantly.

"Go on, roar!" the stranger sneered. He tugged hard on Little Bear's fur.

Little Bear snarled and extended his sharp claws.

"Hush, Little Bear!" the hunters soothed. "Remember what Grandmother told you!"

Quickly, they pushed the stranger away.

But the stranger hissed, "Bears are for eating. Who ever heard of hunters keeping one as a pet? Watch out, animal! One night when your friends are asleep, I shall come to your village and kill you!"

The hunters hurried home to tell Grandmother this terrible news.

She wept bitterly, saying, "Oh dear, Little Bear, it's not safe for you to live in the village any more. Now you are no longer a little cub, you must go out into the wilderness, far away from people, and learn to live all alone — like a real bear."

Little Bear nuzzled Grandmother. He had been very happy living with her in the village but he couldn't wait to learn to live like a real bear at last! So he turned to make his way into the wider world.

"Wait!" Grandmother called.

Hastily, Grandmother dipped her fingers into a pot of oil, and then into some black soot from the fire. She hurried out after Little Bear and gently stroked his side, leaving a large smudge of oily soot on his pure white fur.

Now Little Bear looked completely different from all the other bears.

"Goodbye," whispered Grandmother.

Little Bear nuzzled her one last time. Then he walked eagerly away into the snow.

Grandmother went back into her house and wept all day. When the other villagers heard what had happened, they all wept too, especially the children.

Some people say this story is true; but that is not quite the end of it.

Many years passed. The village boys grew up and became hunters. One day, some of them travelled up into the far north of Greenland, deep into the wildest, most frozen wastelands. There they saw a magnificent polar bear with a large black mark on its flank. It wasn't afraid of them and it didn't attack them. Instead, it came up close and rolled over in the snow like a puppy.

It was Little Bear!

They were all so happy to see him again. Of course, they did not hurt him but left him to enjoy his wilderness in peace.